TO ALL DREAMERS

Lily of the Valley, a Truly Unusual Fairy

Story of the Valley book series

Text, illustrations and design © Zuzana Svobodová, 2024

Creative team: Jacob Svoboda, Lucia Svobodová and Roman Svoboda

Published in 2024 by Writing Doodles LLC

ISBN 978-80-570-5938-7 (Paperback)

ISBN 978-80-570-5937-0 (Hardcover)

ISBN 978-80-570-5939-4 (eBook)

www.zuzanasvobodova.com

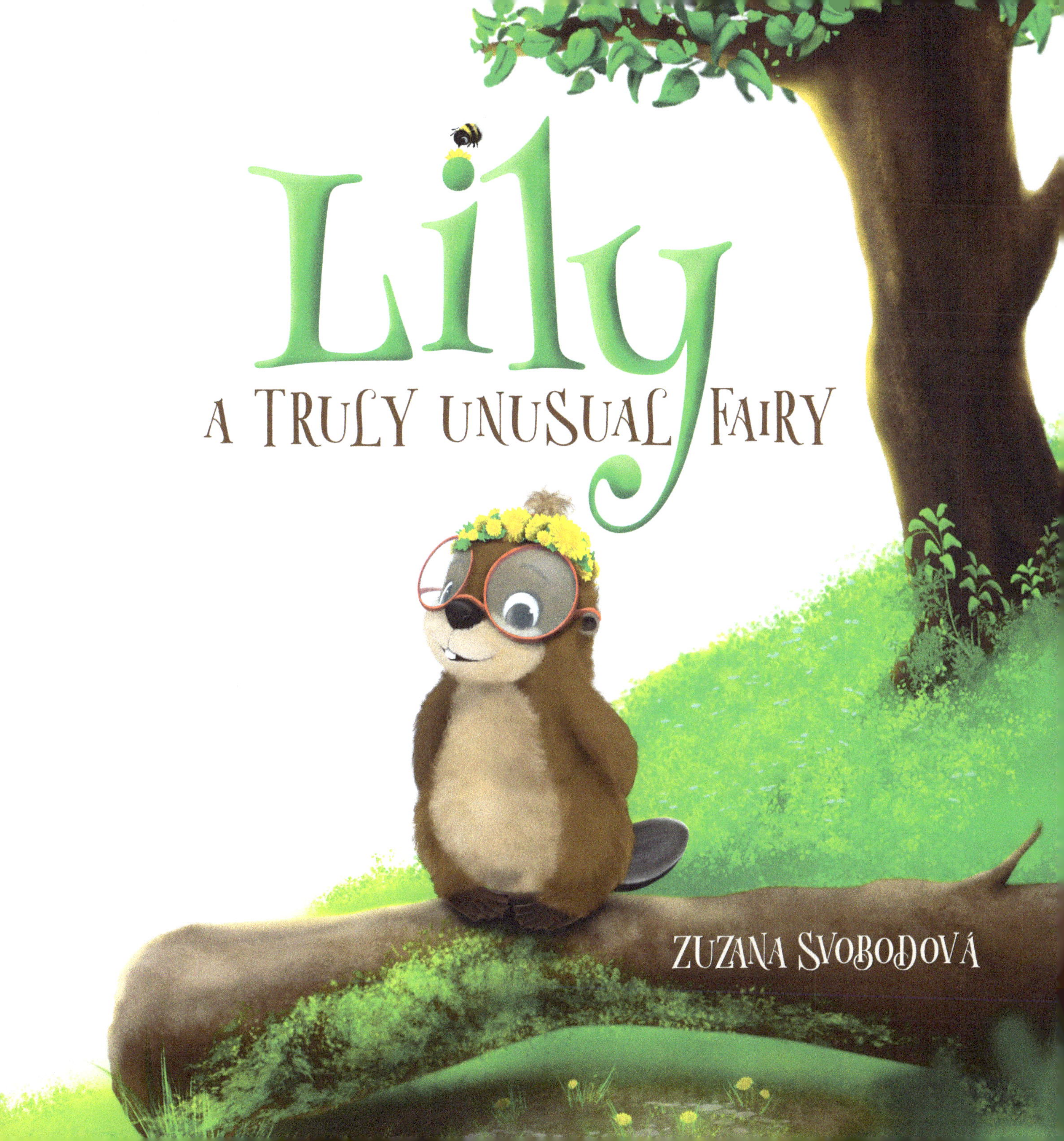

Lily
A TRULY UNUSUAL FAIRY
ZUZANA SVOBODOVÁ

"Fairies, is that you?" a little beaver called Lily whispered,
the breeze blowing the curtains on her window.
The answer was just the drumming of the first raindrops.

"You must exist." Lily looked out at the woods, but only
the shadows of flowers danced in the flickering light of the fireflies.
"I'd love to be one of you," Lily sighed, digging her face deeper
into her palms.

"Lily of the Valley!" a voice came
from behind her.

"I guess we should have named you after another flower because you forget to sleep at night. From now on, I'll call you Forget-me-not." Grandma Juliet smiled, carried Lily to bed and snuggled her up. "I have a fairy story for you," Grandma said with a wink.

As Grandma told Lily a fairy story she hadn't heard before, Lily was amazed.

Her grandma knew so much about fairies; she always had a story to tell.

"Granny, these are such beautiful stories. Fairies enjoy so many adventures.
They are always so kind. I love you telling me about their dandelion wreaths that
they wear on their heads… Look, I drew one today!" Lily opened her sketchbook.
"I would love to be a fairy . . ."

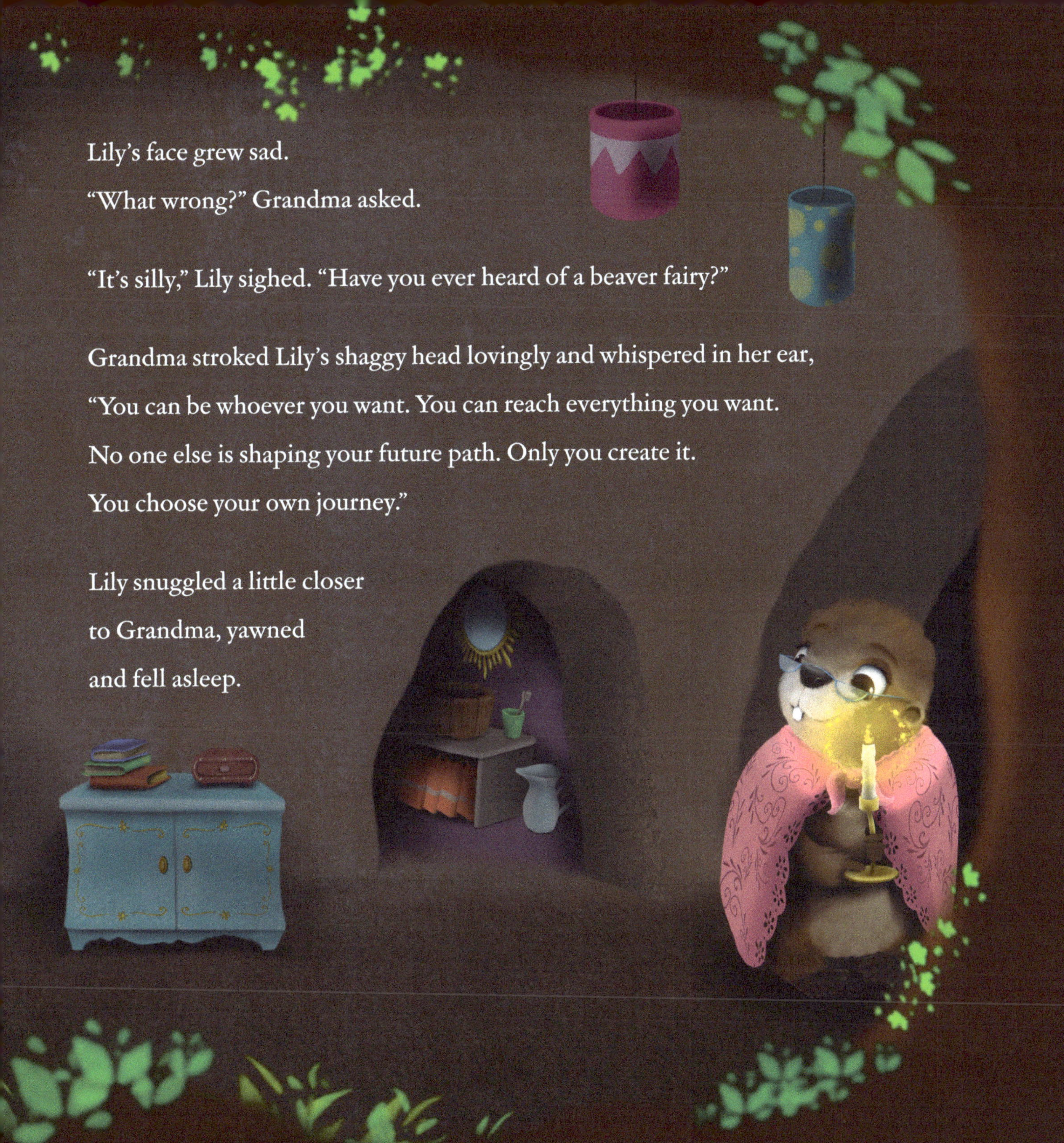

Lily's face grew sad.

"What wrong?" Grandma asked.

"It's silly," Lily sighed. "Have you ever heard of a beaver fairy?"

Grandma stroked Lily's shaggy head lovingly and whispered in her ear,
"You can be whoever you want. You can reach everything you want.
No one else is shaping your future path. Only you create it.
You choose your own journey."

Lily snuggled a little closer
to Grandma, yawned
and fell asleep.

After a night storm, the forest
woke up to a sunny morning.
Lily put a beaded rubber
band in her hair,

grabbed her sketchbook

and ran into the woods.

She was looking forward to meeting her mouse friend Sylvia. "I wonder what Sylvia will say about my new pictures and what news she will have," Lily thought.

Lily's sketchbook was full of fairies and Sylvia Mouse had a notebook full of recipes.
Sylvia wanted to become a famous chef.
"Maybe Sylvia will bring cakes today," Lily thought, stroking her squeaking fluffy belly.

When Lily arrived at the clearing in the forest where she usually
met her friend, Sylvia wasn't there. Lily sat among the flowers
and tried to knit a wreath like the fairies wore in her grandma's stories.
But her fingers were a little clumsy, and her dandelions
kept unraveling. Lily wondered why Sylvia was late.

"Sylvia is always on time . . . maybe she's baking
something yummy and forgot the time."

Lily decided to go to Sylvia's house to find out.
She sang as she walked. She passed through
a birch grove and neared the creek where
the Mouse Family lived.

Lily liked Sylvia's family,
her brother Jack was always
sticky from jam,

and her mom Charlotte made
the best raspberry lemonade.

A loud noise disturbed her
sweet thoughts.

Lily followed the noise
and began to worry.

It was cries of help!

As Lily grew closer, she saw damage from the night storm! A strong stream of river had destroyed an old wooden bridge. Pieces of broken wood floated downstream. It had been the only bridge, and the Mouse Family were trapped on the other side of the river!

Lily ran to help.

A twig here,

a branch there,

and she made the old bridge
look new – with the help
of her strong teeth.

"Thank you!" The mice whistled with happiness and prepared a small celebration for Lily. Sylvia tried out her new recipe for blueberry muffins, and baked the biggest muffin that could fit in her tiny oven.

Lily licked herself after the last bite and said,
"You will definitely become a famous chef.
You bake the best cakes
in the world!"

Sylvia's eyes lit up with pride but then fell sad.
"Have you heard of a mouse that became a Chef? Isn't that just a silly dream?"

Lily brushed a few crumbs from her fur and shook her head.
"Sylvia, your dream isn't silly. You can become who you want . . ."
Lily remembered Grandma's words and a smile returned to the mouse's face.

When Lily left,
Sylvia started baking.

Encouraged by the words of her friend,

she tried brand new recipes and brave combinations.

She whipped, mixed,

whisked, decorated . . .

She was excited as she ran around the kitchen full of yummy smells.

Her brother helped with the tasting, but there was more dough

on his fluffy fur than in his belly!

As Lily made her way home, her belly full,

she crossed the meadow and entered the oak forest.

She noticed a beautiful clearing under the bushy treetops.

The soft grass invited her to take a break. She rolled onto

her back and watched the changing shapes of the clouds.

The sun's rays danced on the leaves and glittered in the last

drops of rain. After a while, strange sounds disturbed her.

She set out to find out what it was – it sounded like crying.

She discovered a small ladybug on the river bank, climbing out of the water.

She wiped her face with her tiny hands, and drops of water

glistened on her red coat.

"Hi, I'm Lily of the Valley," Lily said with a smile.

Ladybug raised her head and sobbed, "I'm Sophie."

"Has something happened to you?" Lily asked gently as she noticed her teary eyes. "Have you been swimming?"

Sophie paused then said, "I have always dreamed of sailing around the world. I've been building this boat out of a nutshell for weeks." Sophie pointed to a wreckage of a nutshell boat trapped in the mud. "And a night storm destroyed it."

Lily took the ladybug carefully in her hand and said softly,
"Don't worry, I'll help you fix the boat.
You will go on your journey!"

Sophie lowered her eyes to the ground and asked
quietly, "Do you think that makes sense?
Isn't it just a funny dream? Other animals
laugh at me and say they've never seen
a ladybug as a sailor."

Lily shook her head sharply. "I don't find it funny. It is amazing and brave. I'll tell you what my granny told me last night – everyone can choose their own journey. You can follow your dream and reach everything you wish."

Sophie smiled gratefully through her tears. Together, they freed the nutshell from the broken branches and repaired it.

When they were done, Sophie pressed a kiss on Lily's
hairy cheek and jumped aboard with renewed joy.
She waved goodbye and set out on the river
for a test cruise. Lily watched for a moment
as her new friend gently sailed on the water.

In the evening with a cup of cocoa, Lily snuggled in a big armchair.

She told her grandma about her adventures.

"You've just told me a fairy story!" Grandma said.

"Have I? How?" Lily wondered, cocoa foam on her nose.

"Everything you did today was very kind.

You're just as kind as the fairies in my stories."

Grandma stroked her cheek proudly.

As the forest faded into

a charming night,

three windows glowed

in the darkness.

Sylvia was busy
creating new recipes.
She had already filled
two more notebooks
since Lily had left.

Sophie was planning her sailing adventure.

She drew up a plan for her trip using old naval maps.

And Lily drew a whole new picture.

There were three special fairies on it - Lily the Beaver, Sylvia the Mouse

and Sophie the Ladybug. All three had dandelion wreaths on their heads.

Early in the morning, the sun peeked out from behind the clouds and tickled Lily's nose. Lily yawned, stretched and went to the bathroom.

However, when she looked in the mirror, she whooped in surprise. She had a beautiful dandelion wreath on her head - exactly as the fairies had in Grandma's stories. The same as she had drawn last night.

With a single long jump . . .

. . . she appeared at the kitchen door. "Granny! Granny! Take a look!
I have a fairy wreath!" she shouted excitedly. "How is it possible?
How did it happen? When did it happen?"
Questions fell from her quickly.

Grandma took her granddaughter's
hand and said, "When I was little,
I was just like you, Lily.
I also believed in fairies.
And I longed to be
one of them."

Grandma walked to
a large closet in the corner.
She stood on a stool and
reached for the top of the closet.

"I have to show you something."
She handed Lily an old hat box.

Lily took it carefully
and opened it.
She gasped.

Lily looked at her grandma in surprise.

"Have you ever met fairies?" she asked with bated breath.

Grandma picked the beautiful old dried dandelion
wreath from the box and smiled mysteriously.
"I see that I owe you another story
from ancient times. The story of
a little beaver who bravely
embarked on her
dream journey . . ."

THE END

BLUEBERRY MUFFINS
RECIPE BY SYLVIA, THE MOUSE CHEF

WHAT YOU NEED FOR 12 MUFFINS:

Dry ingredients

- 200 g all-purpose flour
- 50 g almond flour
- 2 tsp baking powder
- 1/2 tsp baking soda
- pinch of salt
- 1 tsp cinnamon
- optional: vanilla extract, cardamom, lemon peel...

Wet ingredients

- 50 g dates (if you don't use dates, increase the amount of honey)
- 50 g honey or maple syrup (you can add more if you prefer sweeter)
- 1 apple
- 2 large free-range eggs
- 200 ml milk or plant-based milk (I use soya milk without sugar)
- 80 g melted butter or coconut oil (I use plant-based butter)

Plus

- 100 g blueberries (replace them with other favourite berries, raisins or chocolate)

Let's Bake!

1. Pour boiling water over the dates and leave them aside to cool. In the meantime, take the milk and eggs out of the fridge and bring them to room temperature.

2. Preheat the oven to 380°F/190 °C.

3. Combine all dry ingredients in one bowl, and set aside.

4. Drain the dates and peel the apple. If you don't use dates, just grate the apple.

5. Mix the apple with the dates until smooth.

6. In the second bowl, beat the eggs, date-apple mixture, milk and butter until smooth with a spatula or an electric whisk.

7. Add the dry ingredients to the bowl with the wet ingredients and beat with a spatula to combine; be careful not to overbeat.

8. Stir in the blueberries.

9. Fill the muffin tin. If you do not have a silicone or non-stick form, first grease the tin with oil and sprinkle with flour.

10. Bake for about 20 minutes. Insert a skewer info the centre of one muffin – if it comes clean, they are done.

11. Leave to cool for a few minutes.

Enjoy it!

A LITTLE BIT ABOUT ME

Drawing has been an essential part of me since
a toddler. I still keep a child's soul and outlook
on the world, diving into the world of fantasy
and exploring all its incredible corners.
I love reading books and discovering
new stories with my two kids.

I'm a yogi and a passionate lover of cooking.
I always have a cup of good coffee
or a piece of great chocolate nearby.

I hope you enjoyed Lily's story.
Let me know what you thought of the story
and your baking. You can leave a message at:
Instagram: @zuzana_svobodova_illustration
website: www.zuzanasvobodova.com
email: info@zuzanasvobodova.com
or book series Instagram: @storyofthevalleybook

With love,

ZUZANA SVOBODOVÁ

a children's book illustrator and author